Good Medicine

ISBN: 0-9762014-5-3
ISBN: 978-0-9762014-5-8

Published by L'Edge Press
A division of Upside Down Ministries, Inc.
www.upsidedownministries.com
PO Box 2567
Boone, NC 28607

Acknowledgment

My gratitude to God for His Word and to my son-in-law and daughter, Jeff and Libbi Hendley, for their encouragement and time involved in completing this book.

Foreword

From time to time I receive letters of appreciation that bring me joy from one of my five children. For years I have been writing notes of thankfulness and gratitude to my Heavenly Father believing He, too, gets pleasure from His children when they take time to talk or write to Him. Even though God knows our thoughts and hearts, it still pleases Him when we respond to His letter (the Scriptures) with gratitude.

For most of my 85 years God has blessed me with good health. But like David, I have had my days of distress and trouble. So I tell God whatever concerns me. He already knows, enjoys, and desires the "notes" I write about my daily life. David was "a man after God's own heart" as the Psalms so vividly attest. We can also be a woman or a man after God's own heart when we read and respond to His letters: they are truly Good Medicine.

God's prescription is the most effective medicine for His children when taken daily.

This is your personal journal. Underline, highlight or add your thoughts on the lined pages.

A friend of the
"Great Physician"
GRH

Rx: Read at least one page daily—
more as needed. Refill monthly.

The Great Physician

"I know what I am planning for you," says the Lord.
I have good plans for you, not plans to hurt you,
I will give you hope and a good future." Jeremiah 29:11 NCV

Psalm 73:28
But it is good for me to draw near to God:
I have put my trust in the Lord God, that
I may declare all thy works. KJV

Proverbs 16:3
Commit thy works unto the Lord, and
thy thoughts shall be established. KJV

Philippians 4:13
I can do all things through Christ which strengtheneth
me. KJV

Psalm 119:50,71,105,165
This is my comfort in my affliction; for thy word
   hath quickened me.
It is good for me that I have been afflicted; that I
   might learn thy statutes.
Thy word is a lamp unto my feet, and a light unto
   my path.
Great peace have they which love thy law: and
   nothing shall offend them. KJV

Psalm 16:5-6
Lord, you have assigned me my portion and my cup; you
have made my lot secure. The boundary lines have fallen
for me in pleasant places; surely I have a delightful
inheritance. NIV

Day 1: Thoughts and Prayers

_____

_____

_____

_____

_____

_____

_____

_____

_____

_____

_____

_____

_____

_____

_____

_____

_____

Psalm 92:1-2, 5
It is a good thing to give thanks unto the Lord,
and to sing praises unto Thy name, O most High.
To shew forth thy lovingkindness in the
morning, and Thy faithfulness every night.
Oh Lord, how great are thy works!
And thy thoughts are very deep. KJV

Psalm 103:15-18
As for man, his days are like grass, he flourishes like a
flower of the field; the wind blows over it and it is gone,
and its place remembers it no more. But from everlasting
to everlasting the Lord's love is with those who fear him,
and his righteousness with their children's children—with
those who keep his covenant and remember to obey his
precepts. NIV

2 Corinthians 5:17, 20-21
Therefore if any man be in Christ, he is a new creature:
old things are passed away; behold, all things are become
new...Now then we are ambassadors for Christ, as though
God did beseech you by us: we pray you in Christ's stead,
be ye reconciled to God. For he hath made him to be sin
for us, who knew no sin; that we might be made the
righteousness of God in him. KJV

Day 2: Thoughts and Prayers

_____

_____

_____

_____

_____

_____

_____

_____

_____

_____

_____

_____

_____

_____

John 15:4-5
Abide in Me, and I in you. As the branch cannot bear fruit of itself unless it abides in the vine, so neither can you unless you abide in Me.
I am the vine, you are the branches; he who abides in Me and I in him, he bears much fruit, for apart from Me you can do nothing. NASB

Hebrews 12:14
Make every effort to live in peace with all men and to be holy; without holiness no one will see the Lord. NIV

1 John 4:7, 12
Beloved, let us love one another: for love is of God; and every one that loveth is born of God, and knoweth God...No man hath seen God at any time. If we love one another, God dwelleth in us, and his love is perfected in us. KJV

I Peter 2:9
But you are a chosen people, royal priests, a holy nation, a people for God's own possession. You were chosen to tell about the wonderful acts of God, who called you out of darkness into his wonderful light. NCV

Day 3: Thoughts and Prayers

Psalm 104:33-34
I will sing to the Lord as long as I live;
  I will sing praise to my God while I have my being.
May my meditation be sweet to Him;
  I will be glad in the Lord. NKJV

Psalm 35:9-10
And my soul shall be joyful in the Lord: it shall
rejoice in his salvation. All my bones shall say, Lord, who
is like unto thee, which deliverest the poor from him that
is too strong for him, yea, the poor and needy from him
that spoileth him? KJV

Psalm 37:3-5
Trust in the Lord, and do good; so shalt thou
  dwell in the land, and verily thou shalt be fed.
Delight thyself also in the Lord: and he shall give thee
  the desires of thine heart.
Commit thy way unto the Lord; trust also in him;
  and he shall bring it to pass. KJV

John 15:4-5
Abide in Me, and I in you. As the branch cannot bear
fruit of itself unless it abides in the vine, so neither can
you unless you abide in Me. I am the vine, you are the
branches; he who abides in Me and I in him, he bears
much fruit, for apart from Me you can do nothing. NASB

Day 4: Thoughts and Prayers

Lamentations 3:22-26
The Lord's lovingkindness indeed never cease,
  For His compassions never fail.
They are new every morning;
  Great is Thy faithfulness.
"The Lord is my portion," says my soul,
  "Therefore I have hope in Him."
The Lord is good to those who wait for Him,
  To the person who seeks Him.
It is good that he waits silently
  For the salvation of the Lord. NASB

Colossians 3:15-17
And let the peace of Christ rule in your hearts, to which indeed you were called in one body. And be thankful. Let the word of Christ dwell in you richly, teaching and admonishing one another in all wisdom, singing psalms and hymns and spiritual songs, with thankfulness in your hearts to God. And whatever you do, in word or deed, do everything in the name of the Lord Jesus, giving thanks to God the Father through him. ESV

Psalm 34:19
A righteous man may have many troubles but the Lord delivers him from them all. NIV

Day 5: Thoughts and Prayers

_____

_____

_____

_____

_____

_____

_____

_____

_____

_____

_____

_____

_____

_____

Ephesians 3:14-19
My response is to get down on my knees before the Father, this magnificent Father who parcels out all heaven and earth. I ask him to strengthen you by his Spirit—not a brute strength but a glorious inner strength—that Christ will live in you as you open the door and invite him in. And I ask him that with both feet planted firmly on love, you'll be able to take in with all Christians the extravagant dimensions of Christ's love. Reach out and experience the breadth! Test its length! Plumb the depths! Rise to the heights! Live full lives, full in the fullness of God.
The Message

Psalm 62:1-2, 5-6, 8
Truly my soul waiteth upon God: from him cometh
  my salvation.
He only is my rock and my salvation; he is my defense;
  I shall not be greatly moved...
My soul, wait thou only upon God; for my expectation is
  from him.
He only is my rock and my salvation: he is my defense;
  I shall not be moved...
Trust in him at all times; ye people, pour out your heart
  before him: God is a refuge for us. KJV

Isaiah 26:3
You, Lord, give true peace
  to those who depend on you,
  because they trust you. NCV

Day 6: Thoughts and Prayers

Matthew 11:28-29
Come to Me, all who are weary and heavy-laden, and I will give you rest. Take my yoke upon you and learn from Me, for I am gentle and humble in heart, and you will find rest for your souls. NASB

Psalm 34:7-9, 15-18
The angel of the Lord encamps around those who fear him, and he delivers them.
Taste and see that the Lord is good; blessed is the man who takes refuge in him.
Fear the Lord, you his saints, for those who fear him lack nothing...
The eyes of the Lord are on the righteous and his ears are attentive to their cry;
the face of the Lord is against those who do evil, to cut off the memory of them from the earth.
The righteous cry out, and the Lord hears them; he delivers them from all their trouble.
The Lord is close to the brokenhearted and saves those who are crushed in spirit. NIV

Romans 8:28
And we know that all things work together for good to them that love God, to them who are the called according to his purpose. KJV

Day 7: Thoughts and Prayers

2 Corinthians 12:9-10
And He has said to me, "My grace is sufficient for you, for power is perfected in weakness." Most gladly, therefore, I will rather boast about my weaknesses, so that the power of Christ may dwell in me. Therefore I am well content with weaknesses, with insults, with distresses, with persecutions, with difficulties, for Christ's sake; for when I am weak, then I am strong. NASB

1 Thessalonians 5:18
In everything give thanks; for this is the will of God in Christ Jesus for you. NKJV

I Peter 1:6-8
In this you greatly rejoice, though now for a little while you may have had to suffer grief in all kinds of trials. These have come so that your faith—of greater worth than gold, which perishes even though refined by fire—may be proved genuine and may result in praise, glory and honor when Jesus Christ is revealed. Though you have not seen him, you love him; and even though you do not see him now, you believe in him and are filled with an inexpressible and glorious joy. NIV

Day 8: Thoughts and Prayers

Proverbs 3:5-6
Trust in the Lord with all your heart,
   And lean not on your own understanding;
In all your ways acknowledge Him,
   and He will make your paths straight. NIV

I Peter 5:7
Cast all your anxiety on him because he cares for you.
NIV

Psalm 27:5
For he will hide me in his shelter in the day of trouble;
he will conceal me under the cover of his tent; he will lift
me high upon a rock. ESV

Matthew 6:25-26
Therefore I say unto you, Take no thought for your life,
what ye shall eat, or what ye shall drink; nor yet for your
body, what ye shall put on. Is not the life more than
meat, and the body than raiment? Behold the fowls of
the air: for they sow not, neither do they reap, nor
gather into barns; yet your heavenly Father feedeth
them. Are ye not much better than they? KJV

Matthew 11:28-29
Come to Me, all who are weary and heavy-laden, and I
will give you rest. Take my yoke upon you and learn from
Me, for I am gentle and humble in heart, and you will
find rest for your souls. NASB

Day 9: Thoughts and Prayers

_____

_____

_____

_____

_____

_____

_____

_____

_____

_____

_____

_____

_____

_____

I Corinthians 3:16-17

Do you not know that you are a temple of God and that the Spirit of God dwells in you? If any man destroys the temple of God, God will destroy him, for the temple of God is holy, and that is what you are. NASB

Philippians 4:4-9

Rejoice in the Lord always: and again I say, Rejoice. Let your moderation be known unto all men. The Lord is at hand. Be careful for nothing; but in every thing by prayer and supplication with thanksgiving let your requests be made known unto God. And the peace of God, which passeth all understanding, shall keep your hearts and minds through Christ Jesus. Finally, brethren, whatsoever things are <u>true</u>, whatsoever things are <u>honest</u>, whatsoever things are <u>just</u>, whatsoever things are <u>pure</u>, whatsoever things are <u>lovely</u>, whatsoever things are of <u>good</u> <u>report</u>; if there be any <u>virtue</u>, and if there be any <u>praise</u>, <u>think on these things.</u> Those things, which ye have both learned, and received, and heard, and seen in me, do: <u>and the God of peace shall be with you.</u> KJV

1 Thessalonians 1:6-8

You became imitators of us and of the Lord; in spite of severe suffering, you welcomed the message with the joy given by the Holy Spirit. And so you became a model to all the believers in Macedonia and Achaia. The Lord's message rang out from you not only in Macedonia and Achaia—your faith in God has become known everywhere. Therefore we do not need to say anything about it. NIV

Day 10: Thoughts and Prayers

_____

_____

_____

_____

_____

_____

_____

_____

_____

_____

_____

_____

_____

_____

_____

_____

Psalm 16:5-6
Lord, you have assigned me my portion and my cup;
  you have made my lot secure.
The boundary lines have fallen for me in pleasant places;
  surely I have a delightful inheritance. NIV
(This is so true. I have claimed it for years)

Psalm 23: 1-6
The Lord is my shepherd; I shall not want.
He maketh me to lie down in green pastures:
  he leadeth me beside the still waters.
He restoreth my soul: he leadeth me in the paths
  of righteousness for his name's sake.
Yea, though I walk through the valley of the
  shadow of death, I will fear no evil; for thou art
  with me; thy rod and thy staff they comfort me.
Thou preparest a table before me in the presence
  of mine enemies: thou anointest my head with
  oil; my cup runneth over.
Surely goodness and mercy shall follow me all
  the days of my life: and I will dwell in the
  house of the Lord for ever. KJV

I Thessalonians 5:18
In everything give thanks; for this is the will of God in
Christ Jesus for you. NKJV

Day 11: Thoughts and Prayers

Jeremiah 32:41
Yes, I will rejoice over them to do them good, and I will assuredly plant them in this land, with all My heart and with all My soul. NKJV

Psalm 36:7
How precious is Your lovingkindness, O God!
Therefore the children of men put their
trust under the shadow of Your wings. NKJV

Mark 2:17
When Jesus heard it, he saith unto them, They that are whole have no need of the physician, but they that are sick: I came not to call the righteous, but sinners to repentance. KJV

Luke 19:10
For the Son of man is come to seek and to save that which was lost. KJV

Colossians 1:12-14
Giving thanks unto the Father, which hath made us meet to be partakers of the inheritance of the saints in light: who hath delivered us from the power of darkness, and hath translated us into the kingdom of his dear Son: in whom we have redemption through his blood, even the forgiveness of sins. KJV

Day 12: Thoughts and Prayers

_____

_____

_____

_____

_____

_____

_____

_____

_____

_____

_____

_____

_____

_____

_____

Psalm 103:1-5

Bless the Lord, O my soul: and all that is within
me, bless his holy name.
Bless the Lord, O my soul, and forget not all
his benefits:
Who forgiveth all thine iniquities; who healeth all
thy diseases;
Who redeemeth thy life from destruction; who
crowneth thee with lovingkindness and tender mercies;
Who satisfieth thy mouth with good things; so
that thy youth is renewed like the eagles. KJV

Daniel 2:20-23

And said, "Praise be to the name of God for ever and
ever; wisdom and power are his. He changes times and
seasons; he sets up kings and deposes them. He gives
wisdom to the wise and knowledge to the discerning.
He reveals deep and hidden things; he knows what lies
in darkness, and light dwells with him. I thank and praise
you, O God of my fathers: You have given me wisdom
and power, you have made known to me what we asked
of you, you have made known to us the dream of the
king." NIV

Day 13: Thoughts and Prayers

_____

_____

_____

_____

_____

_____

_____

_____

_____

_____

_____

_____

_____

_____

Psalm 13:5-6

But I have trusted in thy mercy; my heart shall
 rejoice in thy salvation.
I will sing unto the Lord, because he hath dealt
 bountifully with me. KJV

Isaiah 46:4

Even to your old age and gray hairs
 I am he, I am he who will sustain you.
 I have made you and I will carry you;
 I will sustain you and I will rescue you. NIV

Psalm 33:1-3

Rejoice in the Lord, O ye righteous:
 for praise is comely for the upright.
Praise the Lord with harp:
 sing unto him with the psaltery and an
 instrument of ten strings.
Sing unto him a new song;
 play skillfully with a loud noise. KJV

I Peter 5:7

Cast all your anxiety on him because he cares for you.
NIV

Philippians 4:7

And God's peace, which is so great we cannot understand
it, will keep your hearts and minds in Christ Jesus. NCV

Day 14: Thoughts and Prayers

_____

_____

_____

_____

_____

_____

_____

_____

_____

_____

_____

_____

_____

_____

Deuteronomy 32:4
He is the Rock, his works are perfect,
    and all his ways are just.
A faithful God who does no wrong,
    upright and just is he. NIV

Hebrews 6:10
For God is not unjust to forget your work and labor of love which you have shown toward His name, in that you have ministered to the saints, and do minister. NKJV

Romans 8:18
For I reckon that the sufferings of this present time are not worthy to be compared with the glory which shall be revealed in us. KJV

John 3:16-18
For God so loved the world, that he gave his only begotton Son, that whosoever believeth in him should not perish, but have everlasting life. For God sent not his Son into the world to condemn the world; but that the world through him might be saved. He that believeth on him is not condemned: but he that believeth not is condemned already, because he hath not believed in the name of the only begotton Son of God. KJV

Day 15: Thoughts and Prayers

_____

_____

_____

_____

_____

_____

_____

_____

_____

_____

_____

_____

_____

_____

Psalm 119:11
Thy word have I hid in mine heart, that I might not sin against thee. KJV

Psalm 139:13-14
For You formed my inward parts;
  You covered me in my mother's womb.
I will praise You, for I am fearfully and wonderfully made;
  Marvelous are Your works,
  And that my soul knows very well. NKJV

I Corinthians 13:1-7
If I speak in the tongues of men and of angels, but have not love, I am only a resounding gong or a clanging cymbal. If I have the gift of prophecy and can fathom all mysteries and all knowledge, and if I have a faith that can move mountains, but have not love, I am nothing. If I give all I possess to the poor and surrender my body to the flames, but have not love, I gain nothing.
Love is patient, love is kind. It does not envy, it does not boast, it is not proud. It is not rude, it is not self-seeking, it is not easily angered, it keeps no record of wrongs. Love does not delight in evil but rejoices with the truth. It always protects, always trusts, always hopes, always perseveres. Love never fails. NIV

Day 16: Thoughts and Prayers

_____

_____

_____

_____

_____

_____

_____

_____

_____

_____

_____

_____

_____

_____

_____

I Peter 4:8
Above all, keep fervent in your love for one another, because love covers a multitude of sins. NASB

I John 3:17-18
But whoever has this world's goods, and sees his brother in need, and shuts up his heart from him, how does the love of God abide in him?
My little children, let us not love in word or in tongue, but in deed and in truth. NKJV

John 15:5, 7-9
I am the vine, ye are the branches: He that abideth in me, and I in him, the same bringeth forth much fruit: for without me ye can do nothing...If ye abide in me, and my words abide in you, ye shall ask what ye will, and it shall be done unto you. Herein is my Father glorified, that ye bear much fruit; so shall ye be my disciples. As the Father hath loved me, so have I loved you: continue ye in my love. KJV

Psalm 36:7
How precious is Your lovingkindness, O God! Therefore the children of men put their trust under the shadow of Your wings. NKJV

Day 17: Thoughts and Prayers

_____

_____

_____

_____

_____

_____

_____

_____

_____

_____

_____

_____

_____

Ephesians 2:10
For we are God's workmanship, created in Christ Jesus to do good works, which God prepared in advance for us to do. NIV

Isaiah 61:10
I delight greatly in the Lord;
   my soul rejoices in my God.
For he has clothed me with garments of salvation
   and arrayed me in a robe of righteousness, as a
   bridegroom adorns his head like a priest, and as
   a bride adorns herself with her jewels. NIV

Ephesians 1:18-21
I pray also that the eyes of your heart may be enlightened in order that you may know the hope to which he has called you, the riches of his glorious inheritance in the saints, and his incomparably great power for us who believe. That power is like the working of his mighty strength, which he exerted in Christ when he raised him from the dead and seated him at his right hand in the heavenly realms, far above all rule and authority, power and dominion, and every title that can be given, not only in the present age but also in the one to come. NIV

Jeremiah 33:3
Call to me and I will answer you, and show you great and mighty things, which you do not know. NKJV

Day 18: Thoughts and Prayers

_____

_____

_____

_____

_____

_____

_____

_____

_____

_____

_____

_____

_____

_____

Romans 8:15-18
For you have not received a spirit of slavery leading to fear again, but you have received a spirit of adoption as sons by which we cry out, "Abba! Father!
The Spirit Himself testifies with our spirit that we are children of God, and if children, heirs also, heirs of God and fellow heirs with Christ, if indeed we suffer with Him in order that we may also be glorified with Him.
For I consider that the sufferings of this present time are not worthy to be compared with the glory that is to be revealed to us. NASB

Psalm 103:13-14
As a father shows compassion to his children,
   so the Lord shows compassion to those who
   fear him.
For he knows our frame;
   he remembers that we are dust. ESV

Isaiah 46:4
Even to your old age and gray hairs
I am he, I am he who will sustain you.
I have made you and I will carry you;
I will sustain you and I will rescue you. NIV

Day 19: Thoughts and Prayers

_____

_____

_____

_____

_____

_____

_____

_____

_____

_____

_____

_____

_____

_____

John 8:12
Then Jesus again spoke to them, saying, "I am the Light of the World; he who follows Me will not walk in the darkness, but will have the Light of life." NASB

John 6:35
And Jesus said to them, "I am the bread of life. He who comes to Me shall never hunger, and he who believes in Me shall never thirst." NKJV

Hebrews 4:14, 16
Seeing then that we have a great high priest, that is passed into the heavens, Jesus the Son of God, let us hold fast our profession...Let us therefore come boldly unto the throne of grace, that we may obtain mercy, and find grace to help in the time of need. KJV

Genesis 1:1
In the beginning God created the heaven and the earth. KJV

John 15:5
I am the vine, ye are the branches: He that abideth in me, and I in him, the same bringeth forth much fruit: for without me ye can do nothing. KJV

Day 20: Thoughts and Prayers

_____

_____

_____

_____

_____

_____

_____

_____

_____

_____

_____

_____

_____

Psalm 121:1-3
A song of ascents. NIV

I lift up my eyes to the hills—
    where does my help come from?
My help comes from the Lord,
    the Maker of heaven and earth.
He will not let your foot slip—
    he who watches over you will not slumber.

Psalm 62:8
Trust in him at all times, ye people, pour out your heart
before him: God is a refuge for us. Selah. KJV

Isaiah 40:31
But they that wait upon the Lord shall renew their strength;
they shall mount up with wings as eagles; they shall run,
and not be weary; and they shall walk, and not faint. KJV

Proverbs 3:5-6
Trust in the Lord with all thine heart; and lean not unto
thine own understanding. In all thy ways acknowledge
him, and he shall direct thy paths. KJV

Philippians 1:9-10
And this I pray, that your love may abound yet more and
more in knowledge and in all judgment; That ye may
approve things that are excellent; that ye may be sincere
and without offence till the day of Christ. KJV

Day 21: Thoughts and Prayers

_____

_____

_____

_____

_____

_____

_____

_____

_____

_____

_____

_____

_____

_____

Psalm 4:7-8
Thou hast put gladness in my heart,
  More than when their grain and new wine abound.
In peace I will both lie down and sleep,
  For Thou alone, O Lord, make me to dwell in safety.
NASB

Hebrews 6:10
God is not unjust; he will not forget your work and the love you have shown him as you have helped his people and continue to help them. NIV

I John 3:18
Dear children, let us not love with words or tongue but with actions and in truth. NIV

Psalm 148:1-5
Praise ye the Lord, Praise ye the Lord from the heavens: praise him in the heights. Praise ye him, all his angels: praise ye him, all his hosts. Praise ye him, sun and moon: praise him, all ye stars of light. Praise him, ye heavens of heavens, and ye waters that be above the heavens. Let them praise the name of the Lord: for he commanded, and they were created. KJV

John 3:16
For God so loved the world, that he gave his only begotten Son, that whosoever believeth in him should not perish, but have everlasting life. KJV

Day 22: Thoughts and Prayers

_____

_____

_____

_____

_____

_____

_____

_____

_____

_____

_____

_____

_____

_____

Hebrews 13:15-16
Therefore by Him let us continually offer the sacrifice of praise to God, that is, the fruit of our lips, giving thanks to His name. But do not forget to do good and to share, for with such sacrifices God is well pleased. NKJV

Ephesians 3:20-21
Now unto him that is able to do exceeding abundantly above all that we ask or think, according to the power that worketh in us, unto him be glory in the church by Christ Jesus throughout all ages, world without end. Amen. KJV

Philippians 1:20-21
According to my earnest expectation and my hope, that in nothing I shall be ashamed, but that with all boldness, as always, so now also Christ shall be magnified in my body, whether it be by life, or by death. For to me to live is Christ, and to die is gain. KJV

Isaiah 32:17-18
The fruit of righteousness will be peace; the effect of righteousness will be quietness and confidence forever. My people will live in peaceful dwelling places, in secure homes, in undisturbed places of rest. NIV

Day 23: Thoughts and Prayers

Romans 11:33-36
Oh, the depth of the riches both of the wisdom and knowledge of God! How unsearchable are His judgments and His ways past finding out.
For who has known the mind of the Lord?
Or who has become His counselor?
Or who has first given to Him
And it shall be repaid to Him?
For of Him and through Him and to Him are all things, to whom be glory forever. Amen. NKJV

Exodus 15:11, 13
Who is like unto thee, O Lord, among the gods? who is like thee, glorious in holiness, fearful in praises, doing wonders?...Thou in thy mercy hast led forth the people which thou hast redeemed: thou hast guided them in thy strength unto thy holy habitation. KJV

Psalm 4:7-8
You have filled my heart with greater joy
    than when their grain and new wine abound.
I will lie down and sleep in peace,
    for you alone, O Lord,
    make me dwell in safety. NIV

Psalm 100:4-5
Enter into his gates with thanksgiving, and into his courts with praise: be thankful unto him, and bless his name. For the LORD is good; his mercy is everlasting; and his truth endureth to all generations. KJV

Day 24: Thoughts and Prayers

_____

_____

_____

_____

_____

_____

_____

_____

_____

_____

_____

_____

_____

_____

Psalm 91:14-16
Because he hath set his love upon me, therefore will I
deliver him: I will set him on high, because he hath
known my name.

He shall call upon me, and I will answer him: I will be with
him in trouble; I will deliver him, and honor him.

With long life will I satisfy him, and shew him my
salvation. KJV

Psalm 37:4-6, 29
Delight thyself also in the Lord: and he shall give thee the
    desires of thine heart.
Commit they way unto the Lord: trust also in him: and he
    shall bring it to pass.
And he shall bring forth thy righteousness as the light,
    and thy judgment as the noonday...
The righteous shall inherit the land, and dwell therein
    for ever. KJV

1 Corinthians 2: 9
But as it is written, Eye hath not seen, nor ear heard,
neither have entered into the heart of man, the things
which God hath prepared for them that love him. KJV

Day 25: Thoughts and Prayers

_____

_____

_____

_____

_____

_____

_____

_____

_____

_____

_____

_____

_____

_____

Psalm 116:1-2
I love the Lord, because he hath heard my voice and
  my supplications.
Because he hath inclined his ear unto me, therefore will I
  call upon him as long as I live. KJV

Psalm 116:5
Gracious is the Lord, and righteous; yea, our God is
merciful. KJV

Psalm 1:1-3
Blessed is the man who walks not in the counsel of
the ungodly,
  Nor stands in the path of sinners,
  Nor sits in the seat of the scornful,
But his delight is in the law of the Lord,
  And in His law he mediates day and night.
He shall be like a tree
  Planted by the rivers of water,
  That brings forth its fruit in its season,
  Whose leaf also shall not wither;
  And whatever he does shall prosper. NKJV

Psalm 119:11-12, 15-16
Thy word have I hid in mine heart,
  that I might not sin against thee.
Blessed art thou, O Lord: teach me thy statutes.
I will meditate in thy precepts,
  and have respect unto thy ways.
I will delight myself in thy statutes:
  I will not forget thy word. KJV

Day 26: Thoughts and Prayers

_____

_____

_____

_____

_____

_____

_____

_____

_____

_____

_____

_____

_____

_____

2 Corinthians 4:17-18

For our light and momentary troubles are achieving for us an eternal glory that far outweighs them all.
So we fix our eyes not on what is seen, but on what is unseen. For what is seen is temporary, but what is unseen is eternal. NIV

Psalm 138:8

The Lord will accomplish what concerns me;
Thy lovingkindness, O Lord, is everlasting;
Do not forsake the works of Thy hands. NASB

Joshua 1:8-9

This Book of the Law shall not depart from your mouth, but you shall meditate in it day and night, that you may observe to do according to all that is written in it. For then you will make your way prosperous, and then you will have good success. Have I not commanded you? Be strong and of good courage; do not be afraid, nor be dismayed, for the LORD your God is with you wherever you go." NKJV

1 Timothy 2:1-4

Therefore I exhort first of all that supplications, prayers, intercessions, and giving of thanks be made for all men, for kings and all who are in authority, that we may lead a quiet and peaceable life in all godliness and reverence. For this is good and acceptable in the sight of God our Savior, who desires all men to be saved and to come to the knowledge of the truth. NKJV

Day 27: Thoughts and Prayers

_____

_____

_____

_____

_____

_____

_____

_____

_____

_____

_____

_____

_____

_____

_____

_____

2 Corinthians 5:1
Now we know that if the earthly tent we live in is destroyed, we have a building from God, an eternal house in heaven, not built by human hands. NIV

Psalm 62:1-2
My soul finds rest in God alone;
   my salvation comes from him.
He alone is my rock and my salvation;
   he is my fortress, I will never be shaken. NIV

James 1:2-5
My brethren, count it all joy when you fall into various trials, knowing that the testing of our faith produces patience. But let patience have its perfect work, that you may be perfect and complete, lacking in nothing. If any of you lacks wisdom, let him ask of God, who gives to all liberally and without reproach, and it will be given to him. NKJV

Romans 8:18
For I reckon that the sufferings of this present time are not worthy to be compared with the glory which shall be revealed unto us. KJV

Day 28: Thoughts and Prayers

Isaiah 40:31
But those who hope in the Lord
   will renew their strength.
   They will soar on wings like eagles;
   they will run and not grow weary,
   they will walk and not be faint. NIV

Matthew 11:28-30
Come unto me, all ye that labor and are heavy laden, and
I will give you rest. Take my yoke upon you, and learn of
me; for I am meek and lowly in heart: and ye shall find
rest unto your souls. For my yoke is easy, and my burden
is light. KJV

Philippians 2:3-4
Let nothing be done through selfish ambition or conceit,
but in lowliness of mind let each esteem others better
than himself. Let each of you look out not only for his
own interests, but also for the interests of others. NKJV

1 Peter 4:8-10
Above all, love each other deeply, because love covers
over a multitude of sins. Offer hospitality to one another
without grumbling. Each one should use whatever gift he
has received to serve others, faithfully administering
God's grace in its various forms. NIV

Day 29: Thoughts and Prayers

_____

_____

_____

_____

_____

_____

_____

_____

_____

_____

_____

_____

_____

_____

Psalm 86:5
You are forgiving and good, O Lord,
   abounding in love to all who call to you. NIV

Psalm 34:7-8
The angel of the Lord encamps around those who fear
him, and he delivers them.
Taste and see that the Lord is good; blessed is the man
who takes refuge in him. NIV

Psalm 139:13-18
For you formed my inward parts; you covered me in my
mother's womb. I will praise you, for I am fearfully and
wonderfully made; marvelous are your works, and that
my soul knows very well. My frame was not hidden from
you, when I was made in secret, and skillfully wrought in
the lowest parts of the earth. Your eyes saw my
substance, being yet unformed. And in your book they all
were written, the days fashioned for me, when as yet
there were none of them. How precious also are your
thoughts to me, O God! How great is the sum of them! If
I should count them, they would be more in number than
the sand; when I awake, I am still with you. NKJV

1 Thessalonians 3:12-13
And the Lord make you to increase and abound in love
one toward another, and toward all men, even as we do
toward you: To the end he may stablish your hearts
unblameable in holiness before God, even our Father, at
the coming of our Lord Jesus Christ with all his saints. KJV

Day 30: Thoughts and Prayers

_____

_____

_____

_____

_____

_____

_____

_____

_____

_____

_____

_____

_____

_____

Psalm 86:5

You are forgiving and good, O Lord, abounding in love to all who call to you. NIV

Psalm 34:7-8

The angel of the Lord encamps around those who fear him, and he delivers them. Taste and see that the Lord is good; blessed is the man who takes refuge in him. NIV

Psalm 139:13-18

For you formed my inward parts; you covered me in my mother's womb. I will praise you, for I am fearfully and wonderfully made; marvelous are your works, and that my soul knows very well. My frame was not hidden from you, when I was made in secret, and skillfully wrought in the lowest parts of the earth. Your eyes saw my substance, being yet unformed. And in your book they all were written, the days fashioned for me, when as yet there were none of them. How precious also are your thoughts to me, O God! How great is the sum of them! If I should count them, they would be more in number than the sand; when I awake, I am still with you. NKJV

Ephesians 3:20-21

Now to him who is able to do exceedingly abundantly above all that we ask or think, according to the power that works in us, to him be glory in the church by Christ Jesus to all generations, forever and ever. Amen. NKJV

Day 31: Thoughts and Prayers

_____

_____

_____

_____

_____

_____

_____

_____

_____

_____

_____

_____

_____

Doubt is the Devil's best tool:
D—devil
O—offends God
U—underestimates God's power
B—binds you to the enemy
T—troubles your mind and spirit

Faith is a Christian's best tool:
F—Freedom from fear and doubt
A—Accept God at His word
I—I will _____
T—Trust God
H—Hope and Heaven

The secret of living is the art of giving...
You can give without loving—
but you can't love without giving.

Contact Information

To get your Good Medicine refill,
follow the instructions below:

Visit the following websites for ordering information:
www.ledgepress.com
www.upsidedownministries.com

You can also send an email to ledgepress@charter.net
jeff@hendleys.net

For orders of *Good Medicine* and other quality books
on building healthy relationships you can visit
L'Edge Press' website or write to us at:

L'Edge Press
PO Box 2567
Boone, NC 28607

If you are in a hurry you can call us at 828.263.9102.

www.ingramcontent.com/pod-product-compliance
Lightning Source LLC
Chambersburg PA
CBHW071848020426
42331CB00007B/1912